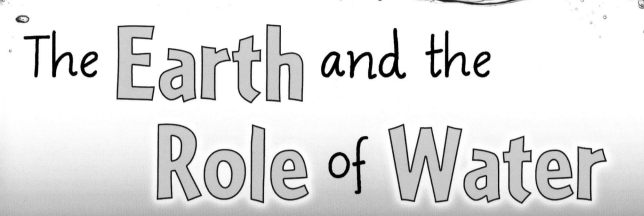

The Earth and the Role of Water

By Shirley Duke

Rourke
Educational Media
rourkeeducationalmedia.com

www.rourkeeducationalmedia.com

PHOTO CREDITS: Cover, title page (top, left to right) © David Joyner, ©Karen Grieve, ©Valentin Casarsa, ©Sam Barnhart, ©Marko Heuver; Table of Contents © Rich Carey; Page 4 © Blue Door Publishing, AridOcean; Page 5 © SunnyS; Page 6 © Alhovik, Zoom Team, Steven Coling, MANDY GODBEHEAR; Page 7 © Filipe B. Varela, Jorg Hackemann; Page 8 © NOAA; Page 9 © Ralf Neumann; Page 10 © Blue Door Publishing, africa924; Page 11 © Anton Balazh; Page 12 © Rozhkovs, Thumbelina, Marcos Carvalho, Andrei Verner, Sadovnikova Olga, Page 13 © Masonjar; Page 14 © Andy Z., NASA; Page 15 © Evgeny Kovalev spb; Page 16 © Matthijs Wetterauw; Page 17 © Blue Door Publishing; Page 18 © Willyam Bradberry; Page 19 © Alexey Stiop; Page 20 © Andrejs Jegorovs; Page 21 © Busfahrer; Page 22 © Adele De Witte, Tomia; Page 23 © Blue Door Publishing; Page 24 © NASA; Page 25 © NASA, artiomp; Page 26/27 © Doug Lemke; Page 27 © mundoview; Page 28 © NASA; Page 29 © hansenn; Page 30 © RedAndr; Page 31 courtesy of NASA, U.S. Navy; Page 30/31 © Rich Carey; Page 33 © Zyankarlo; Page 32/33 © Goodluz; Page 34 © J.D.S., Akeron; Page 35 © funkysoul, Andrey Kekyalyaynen; Page 36 © Chabacano; Page 37 © Pal Teravagimov; Page 38 © Socrates IMWI; Page 39 © paul prescott; Page 40 © 36538936, Miguel Contreras; Page © 41Goran Bogicevic, Alena Brozova; Page 42-43 © Acephotos; Page 43 © Tish1; Page 44 Bruce C. Murray; Page 45 © 83839369

Edited by Precious McKenzie

Cover design by Renee Brady
Layout: Blue Door Publishing, FL

Library of Congress Cataloging-in-Publication Data

The Earth and The Role of Water / Shirley Duke
(Let's Explore Science)
ISBN 978-1-61741-126-6 (hard cover) (alk. paper)
ISBN 978-1-61741-259-1(soft cover)
Library of Congress Control Number: 2011945271

Rourke Educational Media
Printed in the United States of America,
North Mankato, Minnesota

rourkeeducationalmedia.com
customerservice@rourkeeducationalmedia.com • PO Box 643328 Vero Beach, Florida 32964

Table of Contents

CHAPTER ONE

All About Water

Water from the Niagara River plunges 75 feet (23 m) to form the second largest waterfall in the world, Niagara Falls. This river is fed by four of the five Great Lakes. The lakes were carved by Ice Age **glaciers** and hold nearly one-fifth of all the Earth's fresh water.

The fast-moving water scours away tiny particles of rock as it rushes and falls. In 12,500 years, rushing water has worn away the rock. The falls themselves have moved backward seven miles (11.3 km).

The Niagara River continues for fifteen miles (24 km) and empties into Lake Ontario.

Niagara Falls, New York

Niagara Falls is just one of the many awesome examples of the power of water. Without water, in all its forms, people, plants, and animals could not survive.

Water is the only matter found naturally in three different forms: solid, as ice; liquid, as water; and gas, as water vapor. Water freezes at 32 degrees Fahrenheit (0 degrees Celsius) and boils at 212 degrees Fahrenheit (100 degrees Celsius). Water changes form because of changes in temperature.

Freezing water makes it become ice. Warming ice changes it to a liquid again. Boiling releases water as a gas, or vapor, into the air. Cooling water vapor returns it to a liquid state, water.

Water is needed for all life forms. Human bodies are about 60% water. People take in about two and a half quarts (2.4 liters) of water per day. Human brains are 70% water. Blood is 83% water. Cells in the human body move minerals and nutrients in water. Water moves wastes from the human body.

Plants use water to transport nutrients and materials throughout the roots, stems, and leaves. Water evaporates from plants through small openings under their leaves through **transpiration**. They use water in photosynthesis, their food making process.

Transpiration pulls water upward into the plant's roots, stems, and leaves.

People use water in many different ways, such as drinking, cleaning, and cooking. Agriculture, manufacturing, and mining need water. Water generates electricity and provides recreation. Water is vital to life. Yet, one in eight people lack safe drinking water. Careful use of the Earth's water will preserve this most needed resource.

People everywhere in the world need clean water. Scientists think that water is the world's most important resource.

CHAPTER TWO

The Water Cycle

Water is found almost everywhere on Earth. Even the Earth's atmosphere holds water in gas form. This **water vapor** affects the Earth's climate and weather. Changing temperatures cause water to change states, like from rain to snow or lakes drying up in a **drought**.

Heat from the Sun drives the movement of water, known as the water cycle, or **hydrologic cycle**. In the water cycle, water molecules move from the Earth's surface water into the air. Then they return to the surface. Some of the water sinks into the ground. The water continues to move in a cycle, going from the oceans to the air and back to land.

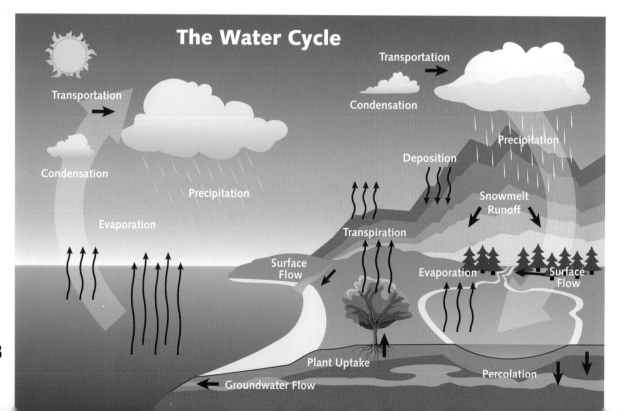

water vapor

As water molecules warm, they rise into the air as water vapor.

The Sun heats bodies of water. Warmer water molecules move faster and bounce off one another. This motion pushes some of them away and into the air as water vapor.

Evaporation occurs when a liquid changes to a gas. Most of the Earth's atmospheric water evaporates from the oceans. A tiny amount comes from rivers and lakes. A small **percentage** of water vapor comes from plants releasing water.

Heat from the Sun causes ocean water to evaporate. The water molecules heat up and move faster. The motion spreads them out. They rise into the air. Air currents carry them higher where the air is much cooler. The water vapor cools, changing from a gas to a liquid. This **condensation** forms little drops, creating clouds.

Over time, the collection of drops becomes too heavy for the air to support. Water falls to the Earth as **precipitation**. Precipitation can be rain, snow, sleet, freezing rain, or hail.

The water from precipitation follows several paths. Some moves across the ground and enters lakes, rivers, and streams. This **runoff** water collects and drains downward. Land where the runoff water collects and then moves toward a single waterway forms a watershed. Watersheds collect precipitation and funnel it to other bodies of water.

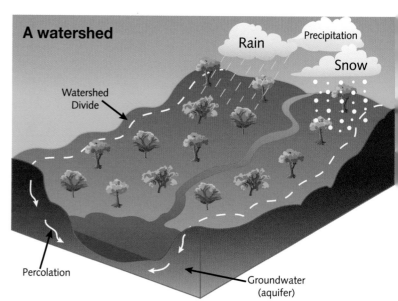

A watershed

Precipitation

Rain

Snow

Watershed
Divide

Percolation

Groundwater
(aquifer)

People without indoor plumbing rely on wells for water.

Water also soaks into the ground. It trickles downward through soil, sand, gravel, and rocks, becoming **groundwater**. This slow, downward movement is called **percolation**. Groundwater collects and pools around **impermeable rock**. Some precipitation evaporates before it ever hits the ground. It becomes water vapor.

From the ocean, the water cycle continues. Sometimes the water is locked up as ice and glaciers. At times during the cycle, people may take the water and use it for their needs. Eventually, it is returned to the water cycle.

The water cycle is a continual, ongoing force on Earth. With wind and the Sun, it creates the weather and climate. The different forms of water act on the land, causing a variety of changes. The cycle continues endlessly, moving water about the Earth.

Land masses usually get more precipitation, while the oceans have more evaporation taking place.

3%

■ Saline Water

Fresh water

97%

*Most of Earth's water is **saline**, or salt water. The remaining water is fresh water, but two thirds of that is ice in the form of glaciers at the poles and in Greenland. Only a small amount of water is actually available for people to use.*

CHAPTER THREE

Water All Around

Surface water is all the fresh and salt water **visible** on the Earth. Most surface water lies in the oceans. Oceans are divided by depth into layers called zones. Different kinds of life live in each zone.

Currents move along the ocean's surface and deep under the water. The currents flow in tracked patterns created by wind, water temperature, the ocean floor shape, and the Earth's rotation.

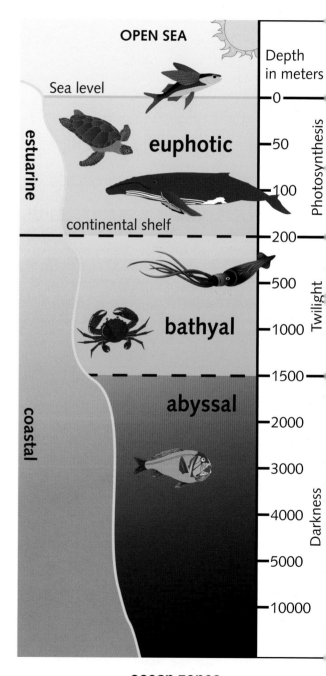

OPEN SEA

Sea level

estuarine

euphotic

continental shelf

coastal

bathyal

abyssal

Depth in meters

0

50

100

200

500

1000

1500

2000

3000

4000

5000

10000

Photosynthesis

Twilight

Darkness

ocean zones
How much light penetrates ocean water determines the zone.

Fresh water makes up around 3% of the Earth's water, but only a fraction of that is usable surface water in rivers or lakes. The rest is ice or it is hidden underground.

Some of Earth's surface water is found as ice in glaciers, year-round snow, and polar ice caps. Ice holds about two percent of Earth's water.

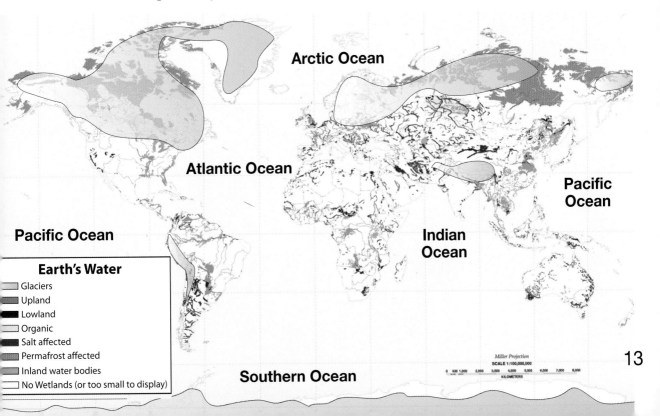

Arctic Ocean

Atlantic Ocean

Pacific Ocean

Pacific Ocean

Indian Ocean

Earth's Water
- Glaciers
- Upland
- Lowland
- Organic
- Salt affected
- Permafrost affected
- Inland water bodies
- No Wetlands (or too small to display)

Southern Ocean

Miller Projection
SCALE 1:100,000,000

0 500 1,000   2,000   3,000   4,000   5,000   6,000   7,000   8,000
KILOMETERS

13

Water surrounded by land creates lakes and ponds. Most lakes are fresh water. Some lakes grow from melting glaciers. Dams form man-made lakes by blocking a river's path.

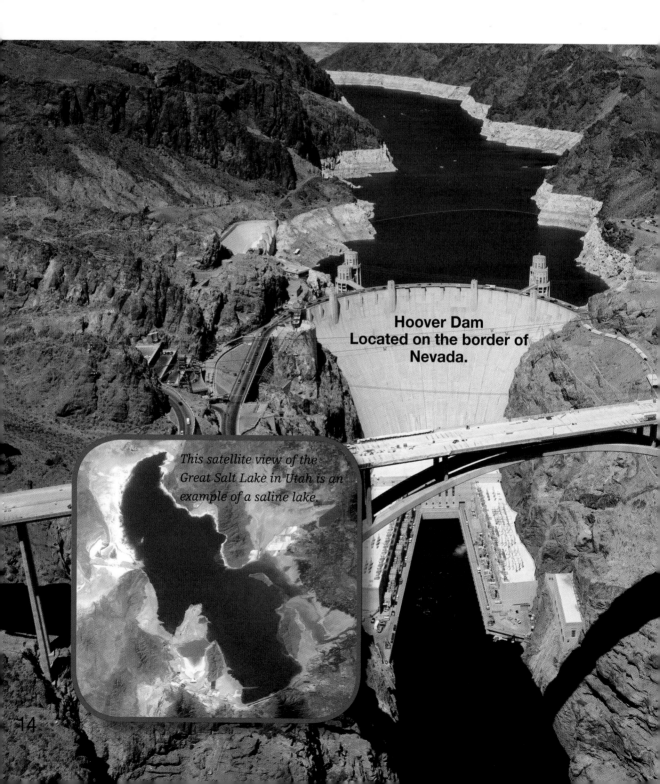

Hoover Dam Located on the border of Nevada.

This satellite view of the Great Salt Lake in Utah is an example of a saline lake.

Wetlands form from standing fresh or salt water. Wetlands include swamps and marshes. Their level of water depends on the seasons, weather, and temperatures.

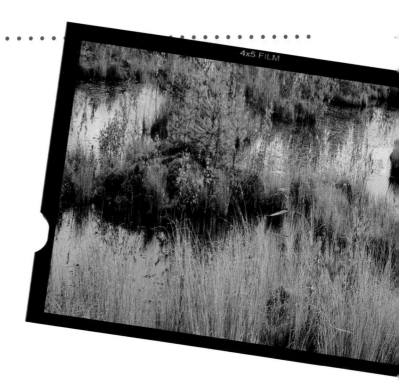

Estuaries are transition regions between fresh water and saline water and support large numbers of life. They serve as a nursery for the eggs and young of many animals, and protect them from battering waves and storm surges. Estuaries offer a resting place for migrating birds and form a buffer zone that helps filter runoff wastes.

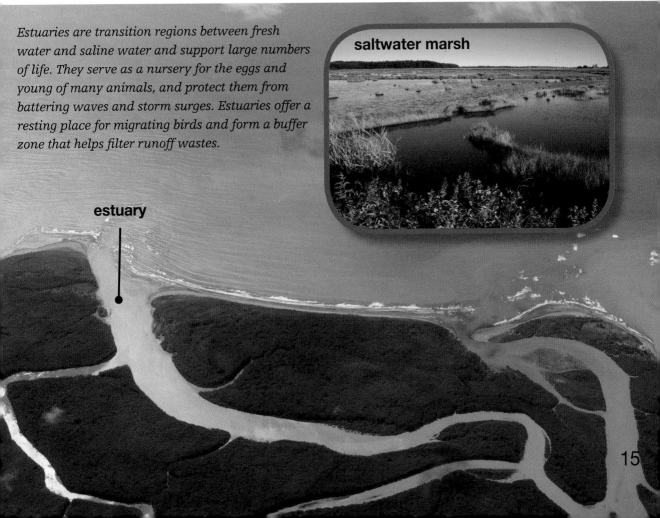

saltwater marsh

estuary

15

Air currents carry water vapor upward to cooler air, where it condenses into clouds.

cool air

cool air

cool air

warm air

Water is also found in the air. Most water vapor is too small to be seen. The amount of water in the air depends on the temperature, winds, the air pressure, and the amount of water vapor already in the air.

Groundwater holds much of the Earth's water. Shallow groundwater is partially refilled by precipitation.

As water seeps downward, the ground is unsaturated, meaning water doesn't fill every space. Rocks are packed more closely deeper down. The water fills every space and then saturates the ground. The line between the unsaturated and saturated groundwater is the water table. It moves up and down because the amount of groundwater changes.

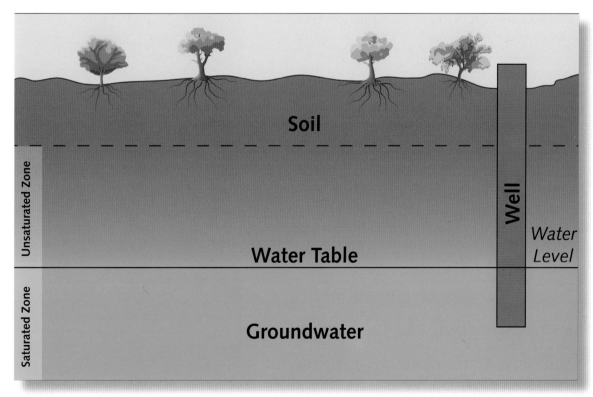

Soil

Unsaturated Zone

Saturated Zone

Water Table

Well

Water Level

Groundwater

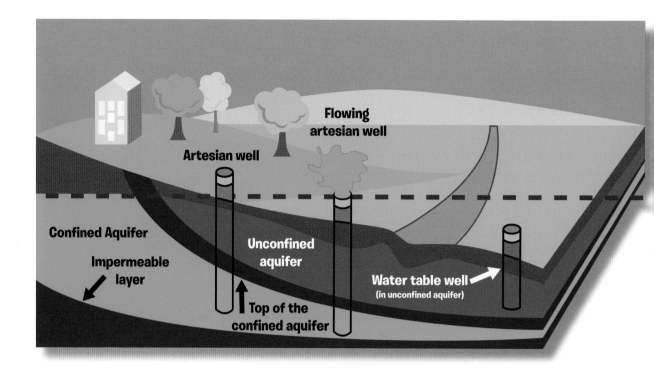

Flowing artesian well

Artesian well

Confined Aquifer

Impermeable layer

Unconfined aquifer

Water table well
(in unconfined aquifer)

Top of the confined aquifer

Areas of groundwater that can't penetrate rock collects in large pools the size of lakes called aquifers. The land above them is **recharged** by precipitation. Water supply companies drill wells into aquifers. Pumps bring the water to the surface.

A confined aquifer encloses water above and below, putting it under pressure. Drilling an artesian well forms an opening and the water will rise upward from its own pressure.

Did You Know?

Salty groundwater collects under oceans and forms aquifers there, too.

Changes in groundwater can cause sinkholes. Sinkholes appear in areas where underground rock is **limestone** or other kinds of soft rock. Spaces and caverns form when the water carries away the dissolved rock. Sometimes the rocks collapse, forming a sinkhole.

The source of the water flowing into the sinkhole is not known for certain. It might be from groundwater in a recharge zone north or east of this area.

Falling water hits the wheel, forcing the wheel to spin.

People put surface water to good use. In the past, moving water turned paddles to run mills to grind corn or cut wood. A modern form of a paddle wheel, a turbine, turns to generate hydropower.

Falling or moving water turns turbines to make electricity. In a generator, magnets turn inside coiled wires to produce electricity.

Something must power the generator so it turns. Some power plants burn fuels, heating water to make steam to turn the generators. Hydropower using falling water, like Niagara Falls, can turn a metal shaft with propellers to generate power.

Hydroelectric Power Dam at the Robert Moses Generating facility, Lewiston, New York.

Did You Know?

During periods of peak flow in the summer and fall, more than 700,000 gallons (2,650,00 liters) of water per second rush over Niagara Falls. That's like filling 35 average size swimming pools in one second!

Dams built along rivers also generate hydropower. Water behind a dam builds up potential energy. The potential energy is changed to mechanical energy by the falling water. The water's force drives the motion to make electricity.

A greater height difference between the incoming water and the outflowing water creates more electricity than using a smaller height difference.

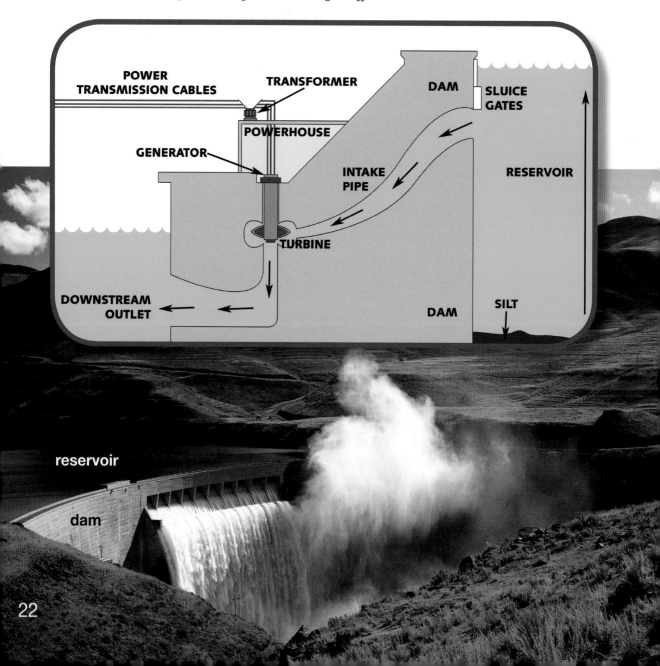

POWER TRANSMISSION CABLES

TRANSFORMER

DAM

SLUICE GATES

POWERHOUSE

GENERATOR

INTAKE PIPE

RESERVOIR

TURBINE

DOWNSTREAM OUTLET

SILT

DAM

reservoir

dam

Hydroelectric power is safe and renewable. Problems however include disrupting wildlife and fish habitats. Migrating fish can't move up rivers blocked by dams. Most of the places for hydropower are already being used. Yet, in the future, cities may have several small hydropower sources generating electricity. Researchers are also looking at generating power using moving tides.

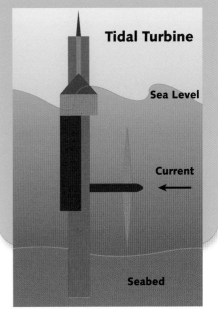

Electrical Power Sources in The United States

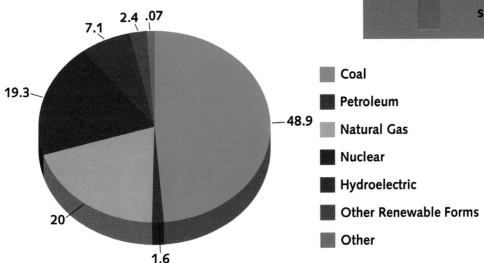

2.4 .07
7.1
19.3
48.9
20
1.6

- Coal
- Petroleum
- Natural Gas
- Nuclear
- Hydroelectric
- Other Renewable Forms
- Other

Scientists are studying Earth's water cycle in order to learn more about how we can better harness water's power. They are also studying water and climate change. Winds, ocean currents, air pressure, the Sun, the Earth's rotation, and the water cycle contribute to the weather and climate on Earth.

Atmospheric water affects climate. Water vapor and other gases in the atmosphere act as greenhouse gases. They reflect sunlight, but hold in heat near the Earth's surface. A warming climate increases evaporation and changes groundwater amounts. Melting glaciers raise ocean levels.

Condensed water vapor forms clouds in the Earth's atmosphere.

Satellite view of Greenland's ice, 1986.

Ice
Ice free

Satellite view of Greenland's ice, 2007.

Ice
Ice free

Scientists are concerned about levels of greenhouse gases and melting ice and those effects on the world's water supply.

GREENHOUSE GASES

Solar energy from the Sun passes through the atmosphere.

Earth's surface is heated by the Sun and radiates the heat back out toward space.

atmosphere

Some energy is reflected back out to space.

Greenhouse gases in the atmosphere trap some of the heat.

CHAPTER FOUR

Water and Erosion

Weathering of rocks by water, wind, and temperature breaks them apart. Chemical weathering by slightly acidic rain dissolves rock. Mechanical weathering occurs when water freezes in cracks. The cracks expand and crumble the rocks over time. Running water rubs against rock with rocks and sand, acting as sandpaper.

Did You Know?

Normal rainwater is close to neutral on the pH scale of acidity. If pollution from industry and cars enters the air, these gases attach to water vapor. This makes the rain more acidic. This acidic water can harm life living in the ponds and lakes where the runoff water goes.

Fast moving rivers push rocks with the water as they flow so that tiny pieces chip off. The tumbling motion smoothes away the rough edges.

Sediments are gravel, rocks, and sand that have been worn away by water, wind, or glaciers. Weathering crumbles rock. **Erosion** wears down rock and also carries it away. Rivers carrying sediments grind away at the land. Riverbeds erode sometimes forming canyons in the land.

An example of a great canyon is the Grand Canyon in Arizona. The Colorado River exposed the rock layers laid down long ago. The cutting force of the water opened up the layers. It took many millions of years to form the Grand Canyon, and it is still eroding!

The Grand Canyon, Arizona

4x5 FILM

220 EPC SSO

Steep sides of these canyons wear down from gravity, rainfall, and landslides. The rivers through the canyons move the sediments and soil. Floods may deposit soil and sediments across the floodplain. The river widens and slows, making larger turns. They deposit the sediments, forming a delta, where they enter the ocean.

Nile River delta, as seen from space.

Other actions cause erosion. Forest fires strip the land of grass and trees that hold the soil. Cutting down forests increases erosion because roots hold soil in place. Precipitation runs off instead of replacing groundwater.

Rain on bare land washes away topsoil exposed by cutting down trees.

CHAPTER FIVE

Weather and Water

Water also causes changes on Earth that have a more dramatic impact than long term erosion and weathering. The water cycle drives the weather, along with extremes in the weather.

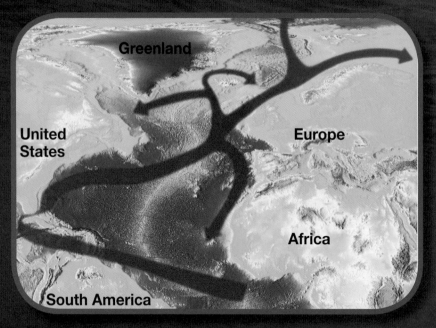

Greenland

United States

Europe

Africa

South America

The Gulf Stream flows along the Southeastern U.S coastline before crossing the Atlantic Ocean, splitting into several branches. It carries warmer waters northward and by Africa, helping moderate or warm the temperatures as it mixes with the colder water.

Ocean currents like the Gulf Stream carry warmer water toward the poles. These currents affect the weather, changing precipitation and temperature on the land nearby.

Hurricane Frances
August 31, 2004

Tropical cyclones are storms with violent wind and rain. Called hurricanes or typhoons, they begin as a mass of low pressure in warm oceans. The mass rotates, gaining strength. This motion moves them, often toward land. The resulting rain and tides flood coastal areas.

Tsunamis result from underwater earthquakes. The motion pushes a large region of water upward. The huge wave of water rushes toward land. The force is unstoppable and sweeps away everything in its path.

The 2011 Japanese tsunami killed tens of thousands people.

4x5 FILM

A drought, a long period of time without rain, dries up crops, withers plants, and causes soil to dry up and blow away. Weather patterns with changes in low and high pressures, air masses stalled by winds in the upper atmosphere, or little water vapor moving upward create drought conditions.

To safeguard against drought, people developed methods to supply water to their crops and livestock. Irrigation supplies water to land using a nearby source brought in by pipes or channels. Careful irrigation increases the amount of usable land for growing food. Lawns, gardens, golf courses, and sports fields are often irrigated. Irrigation, however, reduces resources, affects the water table, and changes ecosystems.

Ancient Romans built open aqueducts to bring water to their cities.

Pont du Gard, a Roman aqueduct in France

CHAPTER SIX

Clean Water for All

Rivers and lakes provide most of the water people use. This water may look clear and clean. However, untreated water contains microscopic germs.

Water Dowsing

Some people claim they can find water by *dowsing* or *divining* for it. They use a forked stick, coat hanger, keys, or other tools to locate water. They hold the forked end in each hand and tilt the straight part upward. When they walk over water the stick moves downward. That's where you should drill. Does it really work? In an area with normal rainfall and rock formations, groundwater will likely be there.

Dowsers, also called water witches or diviners, frequently used traditional forked branches from willow, peach, or witchhazel trees to locate water.

Surface water is not clean. It receives storm water runoff, farming wastes, dumped factory waste, and sometimes septic tank bacteria. Treatment makes this water potable, or safe to drink.

For years, people drilled wells. They pumped groundwater upward by hand. The water that filtered through the ground made it purer than surface water. Today, most city or county water departments or private companies purify and supply clean water for human use.

Public water supply systems take water from nearby rivers, lakes, or wells. Large screens filter it to remove trash and particles. Aeration adds air to remove gases. That improves the taste and smell. Chlorine kills harmful germs.

As water moves through the purification plants, it is tested multiple times. From the first filtering process until it reaches the holding tanks, the water is checked for germs and impurities.

Alum

Ancient Egyptians used alum around 1,500 B.C. to make sediments settle out of their drinking water. Alum is a chemical compound formed by combining aluminum with several other elements.

Next, chemicals like alum are added. This clumps dirt, metal, germs, and particles together. Water sits in tanks until the clumps settle on the bottom. They are removed and the water is filtered again. It's treated for germs once more. From the holding tank, it moves through the pipes past valves and pumps. From there it goes to water tanks, homes, and fire hydrants.

35

Water is stored in holding tanks or water towers. Water towers are placed on the highest ground in the area. Gravity provides pressure, sending water through a series of pipes and pumps. The pipes get smaller as they go, like the way tree branches do. Reducing pipe sizes keeps the water moving. Turning on a faucet allows the water to flow.

Turning on the faucet opens a valve that lets water flow. The valve keeps water from moving backward into the city supply and contaminating it.

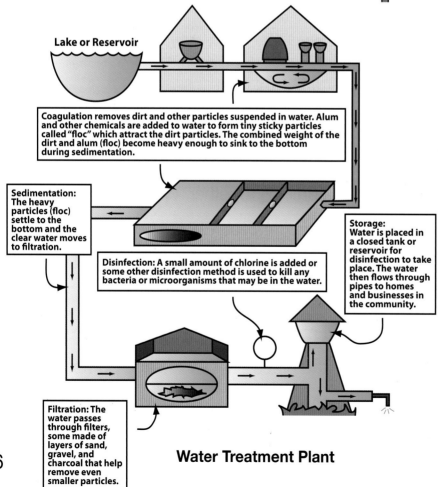

Lake or Reservoir

Coagulation removes dirt and other particles suspended in water. Alum and other chemicals are added to water to form tiny sticky particles called "floc" which attract the dirt particles. The combined weight of the dirt and alum (floc) become heavy enough to sink to the bottom during sedimentation.

Sedimentation: The heavy particles (floc) settle to the bottom and the clear water moves to filtration.

Storage: Water is placed in a closed tank or reservoir for disinfection to take place. The water then flows through pipes to homes and businesses in the community.

Disinfection: A small amount of chlorine is added or some other disinfection method is used to kill any bacteria or microorganisms that may be in the water.

Filtration: The water passes through filters, some made of layers of sand, gravel, and charcoal that help remove even smaller particles.

Water Treatment Plant

Wastewater from kitchens and toilets is treated in sewage plants. It is filtered by stones and then sand. Next, chemicals and light kill germs. That water is usually piped back to large bodies of water. It's not used for drinking water.

Not everyone in the world has potable water. Sometimes the only water source is a polluted, muddy river used by both animals and people. Boiling water or purifying it with 8 drops of bleach per gallon (3.8 liters) of water can make it safe to drink. But not everyone has the materials to do this.

Some people may have water, but no way to purify it, so many people around the world drink, bathe, and wash clothing in water not considered safe.

Lack of money, tools, and knowledge prevents proper sewage treatment. Around the world, 3.5 million people die each year from water-related diseases.

Water is becoming scarcer. By 2025, forty-eight countries will have limited water amounts for daily use. Different organizations are working to provide clean water and sanitation around the world. Conservation of the water supply is vital.

In some countries, open sewage systems containing untreated human and animal wastes infect much of the water, causing diseases such as diarrhea, cholera, and hepatitis A.

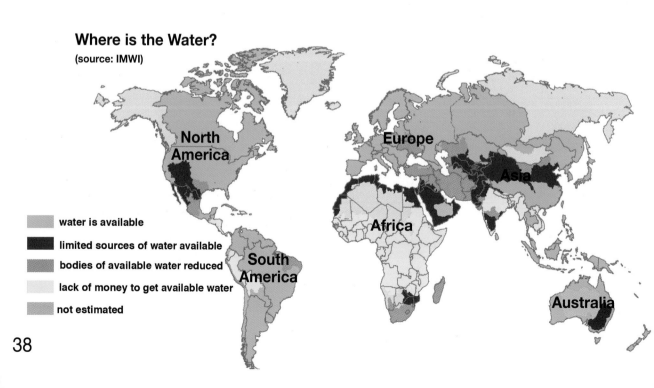

Where is the Water?
(source: IMWI)

North America

Europe

Asia

Africa

South America

Australia

water is available

limited sources of water available

bodies of available water reduced

lack of money to get available water

not estimated

CHAPTER SEVEN

Water for the Future

Developed nations get water different ways. They change rivers, form lakes, and pipe water long distances. The government monitors water quality. Some countries pay for desalinization to make fresh water from salty water.

However, not all nations supply clean water to people. Some women have to walk miles to get water and carry it home. Water treatment plants or water line repairs can't be done because there is not enough money. And, if they do have piped water, that piped water doesn't always flow.

In India, no large city has working water 24 hours a day. In some countries water is very expensive and people can't afford to pay for their water.

39

The need for water will only increase. The world's population is growing. Cities must plan for providing water for their residents. New technology and better sanitation may help.

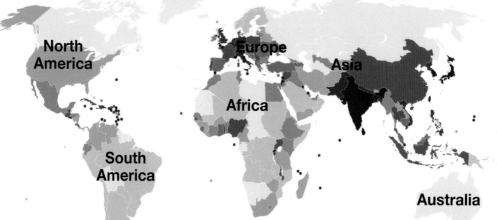

Map showing world population density. Lighter colors represent lesser population density, with the darkest color showing the most densely populated areas.

Half of the world's people live in cities and more are moving to cities every day. People in cities will need more water as the cities grow.

Water For Life

The United Nations developed a plan to reduce the number of people without clean water by 2015. Their goal is to provide drinking water through cooperation among nations. They will fulfill commitments to help fund sustainable water supplies. They also plan to improve sanitation.

Rwanda, Africa

4x5 FILM

220 EPC SSO

Safe drinking water improves public health. People don't get ill from safe, clean water. Education helps people understand ways to conserve, recycle, and use water wisely.

Safe sanitation prevents water pollution by keeping bacteria out of the water supply.

Keeping a **sustainable** water supply is important. This means preserving the current supply of water while dividing it fairly. The water cycle continually moves the world's water. More water can't be used than can be replaced.

Climate changes disrupt typical precipitation amounts. Melting ice caps and glaciers will raise sea levels. Flooding may affect freshwater supplies as coastlines reduce. Changing and unpredictable rainfall patterns hurt farmers' crops.

The continent of Australia is subtropical and the dry air in that region of the world creates low, irregular amounts of rain. Dry weather patterns are also influenced by El Niño, a weather pattern that causes a rise in sea temperatures and weak, easterly winds that push rain clouds away from Australia.

Nations with enough water today may have less water in the future. Research may find ways to use cheaper methods of purifying water using less energy. Planning for the future will ensure enough water is available.

Technology offers some new ways to provide clean water. Bacteria that break down some toxins were discovered. New materials filter water better. Nanotechnology, building materials from the atomic level, may create new materials and better ways to remove salt from water. Improved irrigation systems limit erosion and runoff. Underground and drip irrigation systems reduce water loss.

Some systems run on electric or oil motors instead of water pressure. They spray the water much lower than before, reducing evaporation.

Communities and cities must plan for the future. Water departments can set limits on water use, especially for landscaping. Drought-resistant, native plants survive better in dry regions and need less water to thrive. Conserving water helps protect the water supply and cuts down on wastewater.

Xeriscaping yards by using native plants, mulches, and high quality irrigation protects the environment while saving water.

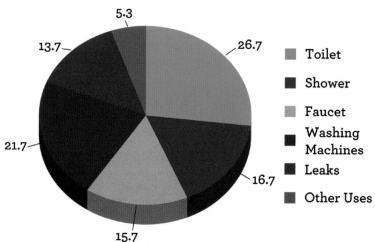

■	Toilet
■	Shower
■	Faucet
■	Washing Machines
■	Leaks
■	Other Uses

Did You Know?

Installing toilets that use reduced amounts of water saves gallons of water every day. Laws in many places limit how fast the water can flow out of faucets, shower heads, and toilets.

Reducing wastewater keeps waterways and sources of usable water as clean as possible.

WHAT CAN YOU DO?

1. Repair all leaks.
2. Shorten showers.
3. Run washing machines and dishwashers only when full.
4. Turn off the water while brushing your teeth until you need to rinse.
5. Rinse dishes in a plugged sink.
6. Water the lawn less.
7. Use local, native plants as landscaping.
8. Install low- flow toilets and faucets.

The same amount of water that has always been on Earth is still here. The problem lies in taking care of this natural resource. Wisely protecting the water supply today will ensure that everyone will have a supply of fresh, clean water to drink now and in the future.

People are working together to help people without enough clean water.

Glossary

condensation (kahn-den-SAY-shuhn): the process of changing from a gas, such as water vapor, to a liquid

drought (drout): a period of time with no precipitation

erosion (i-ROH-zhuhn): wearing away of rock by wind or water

evaporation (i-VAP-uh-ray-zhuhn): the process of changing from a liquid to a gas

glaciers (GLAY-shurz): huge sheets of ice found in the polar regions

groundwater (GROUND-waw-tur): water deposited by precipitation that has trickled into the soil and rocks beneath the Earth's surface

hydrologic cycle (hye-droh-LAH-jik SYE-kuhl): the water cycle, the system where water moves from a liquid to a gas and on cooling, back to liquid

impermeable (im-PUR-mee-uh-buhl): cannot be penetrated by liquids

limestone (LIME-stohn): a hard rock formed from the remains of shells or coral

percentage (pur-SEN-tij): a part considered in relationship to the whole

percolation (PER-koh-lay-zhuhn): a liquid trickling slowly downward through a layer of material

precipitation (pri-sip-i-TAY-shuhn): water or a frozen form of water falling from the sky

recharged (RI-charjd): region where water soaks into the ground to refill an underground supply

runoff (RUHN-off): water that enters a waterway rather than soaking into the ground

sustainable (suh-STAY-nuh-buhl): a process that can continue without using up resources

transpiration (tran-spuh-RAY-shuhn): plants give off water from openings in their leaves in this process

visible (VIZ-uh-buhl): able to be seen

wetlands (WET-luhndz): marshy lands

Index

Websites to Visit

www.epa.gov/owow/NPS/kids/

www.noaa.gov/wx.html

www.water.weather.gov/ahps/

About the Author

Shirley Duke has loved science all her life and taught it for many years. Now she's teaching by writing books. This is her eleventh book. She lives in Texas and New Mexico, where she learned quite a bit about droughts.

Ask The Author!
www.rem4students.com